Terminal Diagrams

Garrick Davis

terminal diagrams

poems

SWALLOW PRESS
ATHENS, OHIO

Swallow Press / Ohio University Press, Athens, Ohio 45701
www.ohioswallow.com

Printed in the United States of America
Swallow Press / Ohio University Press books
are printed on acid-free paper ⊚ ™

18 17 16 15 14 13 12 11 10   5 4 3 2 1

Cover photograph by James D. Steele
Cover design by Beth Pratt

The author would like to acknowledge the following magazines in which, sometimes
in earlier or altered versions, these pieces appeared:

Verse: "Ultramodern"

The Potomac Review: "While Reading the Revelation of St. John the
Divine, I Turn On the Television"

Drunken Boat: "West Hollywood," "Night High above the Los Angeles
Basin"

Library of Congress Cataloging-in-Publication Data
Davis, Garrick.
  Terminal diagrams : poems / Garrick Davis.
    p. cm.
  Includes bibliographical references.
  ISBN 978-0-8040-1130-3 (alk. paper) — ISBN 978-0-8040-1131-0 (pbk. : alk.
paper) — ISBN 978-0-8040-4044-0 (electronic)
  I. Title.
  PS3604.A95696T47 2010
  811'.6—dc22

                                                              2010024346

All sane affirmative speech,

Had been soiled, profaned, debased

To a horrid mechanical screech,

No civil style survived

That pandaemonium

But the wry, the sotto-voce,

Ironic and monochrome

In this association with machinery will probably be found the specific differentiating quality of the new art. It is difficult to define properly at the present moment what this relation to machinery will be. It has nothing whatever to do with the superficial notion that one must beautify machinery. It is not a question of dealing with machinery in the spirit, and with the methods of existing art, but of the creation of a new art having an organisation, and governed by principles, which are at present exemplified unintentionally, as it were, in machinery. It is hardly necessary to repeat at this stage of the argument, that it will not aim at the satisfaction of that particular mental need, which in a vital art results in the production of what is called beauty.

Contents

Solitudinem faciunt, pacem appellant

I.

Everywhere, telephones are ringing
And answered by people paid
To sit and wait for someone to speak

But when the clock says they can leave,
They listen.
It is evening.

Dusk light, strained through smog,
Through radioactive dust
In the upper atmospheres,

Sours the rush-hour crush of cars.
A brown wind strafes the bay.
Each day alters the molecules.

II.

The business suits board and fall
From a sky of beige desks.
The office towers are petrified banknotes.

Say it. Say it. I can't.
Say what the stutter
Of the freeway lamps might mean

Before their sodium tongues halt.
Before all the pre-set timers
Switch night to utter asphalt . . .

III.

On some lush green Argentine hill
The sheep disappear, frequently,
In the clear hiss of gamma rays . . .

The shepherds find their burnt shadows.
"Chlorofluorocarbons!" the papers say.
A man, walking to work, explodes.

"Spontaneous Combustion!"
The papers claim.
But it is something, something else

Passing the depleted ozone.
Like the blond boy birthed from a goat,
Who smiles from the checkout rack

From a paparazzo's photograph
And the tabloid line pleads,
"This Is Not A Hoax!"

IV.

The daily symphony proceeds:
The shift of pedals and angry horns
That play iron grates as cymbals

To accent the fax-machine hum
And click of calculator keys
Ended by slammed file drawers . . .

The flapping pages like a flight of birds
At the disconnect, when choirs
Of answering-machine monologues

Drone that no one is here anymore.
And over all the alarms, faint muzak
Piped through the office as false calm.

V.

Anyway, anyway, what prizes
Do we have for our contestants?
Silence in the cathode showers.

As the applause sign cues
A cowed audience, in the daze
Of flashbulbs and camera angles,

The laugh-track is tripped and sends
Its canned cheer in timely bursts
To synchronize the laughter of the dens.

A greater silence in the heavens.
As roof aerials, like wire crosses,
Triangulate the manna of commercials

In the condominiums,
From the endless rain of money
The billboard-stalks all rise and read:

"The land of milk and honey."
Brand-new, ubiquitous,
The lie on which they all agree.

VI.

It was supposed to be a dream.
It was supposed to be
A paradise with all the sins

We were accustomed to,
And would not quit—
Like the slums of New Jerusalem.

A heaven without the expense
Of damnation and consequence,
And all the best appliances . . .

4

VII.

The remote control shorts and scrambles.
Useless, the tone and color knobs.
A picture waves between channels.

A silicone tit stiffens, to haunt
A game show. The dark roots of dyed hair
Stir before a station-break . . .

Either the images melt or come true.
Scars on liposuctioned hips
Turn orange from tanning booths.

Needle-marks dot such perfect lips.
These pre-fabricated faces
Cannot survive the wrecking ball.

VIII.

Again, traffic, the morning exodus.
Metallic clouds burn the windshields
And all the stoplights are asynchronous.

Something in the distance stalks them.
They merge, but no one yields.
All the car horns are blown, are stuck open.

The credit cards freeze mid-purchase
At every point-of-sale machine.
Colors burn beyond the prism.

Today is a pyramid scheme.
Even the rainbows are corrupt.
And all the car radios sing:

"Our dreams have all gone up on sale,
On tomorrow's pages.
And we pay for the cross and the nails . . ."

And now, at dawn, the moon rises. Red. Wrong.
Whether it was a minute or a year,
Another false millennium . . .

Who shall stand in the wrath to come?

Those days, in their blue apartments, passed
With my heart's dominatrix, in whose arms
I listened to bums ransacking trash
And the weeping of the car alarms . . .

Burned this inky rune upon my idyll.

At the absinthe-hour, I scribble these lines
And lounge where Villon and Verlaine would drink—
A black-leather dandy of nightclubbing.
Who shall explain to you my careless rhymes?

Shall this ink-stained napkin storm the papers?
At best, my sins shall grace some dull review.
My circle? A gang of thieves and strippers
That even I will thrice deny I knew.

Always the same, always the false dawn,
The strobe-light splendor of my salon—
Where nine pale nymphs, wearing sackcloth and ash,

And damning this age that they can't console,
Tear my verse, as penance, in the trash—
And I, an orphan of the oracle.

With her, I worked one humdrum day
    In the dusk of our office den,
Where we dreamed of a brand-new spray
    To halt the spreading of salesmen.

Through flashing rows of strange machines
    We tore pages like memories.
I loved her then, her desperate soul,
    And took her down a grassy knoll.

My compass point rose north from south
    And quenched, quite molten, all too soon
The scented fire of her pink mouth
    In the sweet precession of the moon.

An earthquake came and shook the heart,
    Decreeing we should never part
And so we left, and laughed through town
    While all the world was breaking down.

We fell and, falling, knew we'd leapt
    Into one haven that was ours,
And did not care where we were swept
    Between the gutter and the stars.

Inside those loud, still-blinking screens
        I'd lived for years with copied dreams.
What could I see in what remained?
        She was silence, and the silence named.

Up the staircase, past the jazz band,
New girl, bar tab, beer in hand,
To where old disco splashes kitsch
On dark walls, at migraine pitch.

Switch to break-beats, back to cocktails,
Fine legs, bare waist, polished nails,
And, then, she whispers that I might
Just have her, finally, tonight.

Wait for last call, tip the barmen,
Closed door, lights out, drunk again,
And walk out alone, and older,
To the dawn . . . which held my shoulder.

These blips and beeps,
   Instead of notes, one hears
Are a machine's conceits,
   A muzak-of-the-spheres.
Spaced and arranged
   Like dots upon a grid
Without a tempo change
   Or rhythmic slip.
Each, a strange frequency
   From some fatal star
Sent to conjure
   A kind of *futuristic noir*
To which club dancers jerk and coil
   Or grind their hips
The way worn gears and pistons toil
   In surge and flux.
Each piece of wax propels
   Such fury from within
Until all flesh and metal melds:
   Machines-for-feeling-in.
As if the metronome
   Cannot be stopped,
Re-set, or slowed,
   A Doomsday clock.

Maddening, maddeningly
      Violent, the scene
Of this imposition,
      The patterned trance—

The pre-millennial tension.

Aubade

Morning is when the appliances wake,
And they start me. Outside, I hear
The chirping of helicopters
Above branched tangles of telephone wires . . .

But the cry of dawn's watch is beeping.
Last night, together, we were cold
And lovely in a compliant way.
Parting, your mouth forms its O
In sad silence as flesh deflates . . .

When you left, the hair dryer was screaming.
As now, I pass through blue fields of carpet
And think of your sprawled legs
And wide-eyed stare, a glazed glare
So stable it cannot decay.

Time is lost in the fabric of your beauty.
It is impotent, like the city's coughing.
As wind that shakes the chain-link fences.
As this day, emptied with the dishwasher,
Whose constant churn and gurgle

Rinses nothing clean.
Folded, you wait for me, hissing

Where love's nail snagged a hole.
Angry, I unplug and blow
Until we are both ourselves. Unconsoled,

I tire of the chatter and metal.
But you were sculpted for these streets,
Whose screech you sigh when we rub hard.
You are a piece of its mirror,
In which I can't see anyone alive.

Techno

A jolt shakes an echo from the haze
Of sirens and, *boom,* thunderous bass
Begins to beat and shake the room as bombs
Carpet-dropped, in tempo, during war
Would sound, in an air raid, as a song.

Synthesizers rearrange the roar
Of battle, as drums for melodies
Of dial tones mixed with factory whistles
And error beeps from computer keys
That launched the screaming of the missiles.

Like metal shards, piano-hammered,
The chorus detonates with a voice
Crying from some strip-mall wilderness
Of the new ecstasy-from-violence
While raving kids danced to each dark noise.

Driving ninety miles an hour
To the whine of western music,
I steer for countryside
Or what is left of it,
Since I speed so fast the scenery blurs
Like a photograph. I pass a valley
Of tract houses, where one warehouse
Unstores fire, as a chemical spill
From an overturned truck
Seeps toward the fields
Of a nearby farm where cows cry,
Hooked to milking machines.
Detoured, I breathed in deep
The carcinogenic fumes
And sped on, but nowhere I drove
Could I escape the horizon's
Fine thread of telephone lines.

Tonight, the moon's gray spots
Are the fresh asphalt of mall parking lots.

Past slight shutters, seen through reams
Of his poorly xeroxed dreams,
A paradise bathes him in white
Beyond the spectrum of the desk-lamp light.

Upset, he leaves his telephone voice
And job in the empty office spaces
To chase after figures in the clouds.
An accident, that he is still human . . .

In a world without revelation
Or repentance, where he has no model
And no place, but where the bills arrive
And remind of each lie's obligation.

A life systemized to smother dreams
That, briefly, brought grace
To his most convenient gestures
And brokered face where, once, there was a man.

Cost-Benefit Analysis

When journalists finally came to see
The bald children, diagnosed as dying
From a rare disease, who all came coughing
From playgrounds near the factory,

Spokesmen assured the news no correlation
And brought respected scientists
(Funded at the company's expense)
To say the plant "complied with regulation."

Still, the oozing sores persisted.
And though the plant was soon renamed,
The town's death-rate never changed
As all the publicists had insisted.

So, a grand jury could conclude
"Health risks should affect business aims"
And grant the family lawsuit claims,
Which was expensive . . . for a week or two.

As, somewhere, perched over this death and wrong,
One man crunched the numbers, set costs,
And signed a waiver for the loss
And, from his cubicle, knew all along.

An airplane crashed tonight
Onto the evening news. Each piece
Of charred flesh was cradled
By camera crews, while mothers
Were held back behind police.

The relatives of these corpses
Are interviewed. Soon, all those lives
Are sold, copyrighted, released,
So that actors, with trite dialogue,
Can ride the headline-of-the-week.

All interested parties reimbursed,
All sobbing hushed by settlement,
The funerals seem wrong, rehearsed.
Instead, the children of the dead
Will be raised on insurance claims,

Since these bodies smeared on steel,
These shredded arms on shell gratings,
Will sell movies, book deals,
And boost television ratings.
They have mass market appeal.

The falling ash from the great furnaces
Was once paper, whose train advanced such flesh
As, marked for shipment, held the signature
Of this slight, balding man behind a desk.

Touring the front, where yellow stars fed
A fountain of blood, which sprung from a ditch,
His nausea advanced the treatment line
From bullets to gassing trucks to camps . . .

Even his weakness perfected design.
Perfect cog of the death-machine!
Billing the corpse to pay for its transport . . .

Ignore the noose, because your methods won
In every office, where the drones
Now stamp to numbered files all flesh and blood.

I heard the voice of Hell in this:
The drums so cold and pitiless
That rose, with fire and dragon-wail,
To mock the bloodstained priests of Baal.

Another achromatic night
Limped along the boulevard
Before her heels' whip-crack
Soldered eyes to stockings, hard.
As flames, her hair had curled
And burned: an acetylene torch
Where faces longed to tangle, writhe
Delirious and scorched.
While laughter snapped long lashes
On each yearning eye, as she passed,
That rode her gorgeous, crossed legs
Like a freeway overpass.
She, such a luxury,
Wore pale, unblemished skin
To accessorize in a pose
And photograph—a mannequin
As perfect as vacation,
Or the brand-name of a toy
In the blue of the billboard sky,
As perfect as a marketing ploy.
With eyes like shopping windows
Where all merchandise was backed
By that smile, that vulgar guarantee,
Since her beauty was brute fact.

Still, to see her was to know her
As lovers in pornography

Where sex at obtuse angles
Becomes commodity.
To see her was to own her
As bees, in amber, own their honey.
Just as red, vulgar lips
Were money, money, money.

With her, I spent an indolent sun
Far from the shade of our desks,
Where her flimsy summer dress
Fell, kimono of the courtesan.

Mistakes inside a steel tableau,
We touched and did not ask how soon
Eyes would police to overthrow
This gauze of lips at violent noon.

With her, the glass-and-girder heights
Were lanterns in a stone garden
Arranged purely to delight
Her, pale empress from a far island.

At the intersection of two freeways
Where template curves of concrete
Rise over shopping mall landscapes,
The hum of traffic tunes the pillars

As the arched ribs of cathedrals.
This bridge bears tonight's procession
Of passing red and white lanterns
As the advent of the candles.

Drive Song

At dawn, the first commuters yawn
From bed to desk in succession.
One hears their weak valves stall. At the stoplights,
At the intersections.

Between coffee, bagel, and bill,
The boss yelling, and the heart pill,
The secretary's thigh, and a vast night
Which comes without schedule . . .

After the late taxes, winter,
The silent wife serving dinner
And children known only by telephone
In far cities, and gone . . .

What has this life done, or undone?
The halt and hop of rush hour drones a song . . .
What do the tires on pavement hum?
An automaton, an automaton.

Charged and mortgaged to the marrow,
How are they freed, or found, to live again?

When even the interest narrows,
When even old sitcoms can console them?

At dusk, the same commuters flush
From desk to bed in long delays.
One hears them fold, at last, their sighs muffled
Their choked tears in driveways.

Passing over the Suburbs of San Diego

From an airplane, the canyons veined with blue—
And the decadence of each drained swimming pool.

The Art of Drifting through Los Angeles

Caught in the matrix of streetlights
That I drove through, passing each night
In its cul-de-sac, deciphering
The secret language of graffiti,

Whose spray-painted hieroglyphs blurred
Along the concrete flood-washes,
As the endless suburbs merged
In mean rows streaked with litter . . .

Driving my car hour upon hour,
I drew each route upon a map
To see what the ritual made me:
A strange shape in the city's square blocks.

My art was drifting randomly
Through the traffic signs sheathed in smog
Which all read: DO NOT ENTER/WRONG WAY
Past which it was forbidden to go.

Here, where only celebrities
Could breathe without suffocating,
I tried to escape chained miles of fence
Which could not be breached or fought against.

So was it hallucination
Or did I pass through the sour fog
Of breweries, and gleaming warehouse dens,
And see men clothed in newspaper shreds?

Was it dream or just reflection
When I passed a chrome tanker, stalled
Beside the road, and its driver still
By the red shadow on his crushed grille?

Was the blood just an accident
That I drove through, as it sizzled
In the white-hot core of the road flare?
As cars slowed down, not to help, but stare?

"Useless," I screamed and drove on.
But no elaborate game could make
The earthquakes shift and miss. Nothing now
Could turn the jagged patterns seamless.

There never was an accident,
According to the evening news,
Inside this grid of white-washed boxes,
This warren of crowded solitudes.

But something almost infinite
Was spilled on the contours of that road,

Something planners could not make perfect
Now spread to the edges of the world.

There, inside my composition,
I saw how the world was undone;
The ruined outline, drawn with precision,
And the naked man haloed in blood.

Etiwanda

A train-track grid staples dawn
To the shifting sheet of dirt
In a thousand factory yards.
Grease smears the four corners of the earth.

On Passing the San Onofre Nuclear Power Plant

They drive over her buried waist
On the asphalt belt of freeway,
Near white, lead tanks of waste
Like bottles of suntan lotion
Dropped by her slender fuel-pumps . . .

Near two steel loading cranes
That hang as hands to heavy water,
Each bent arm statuesque,
While brushing from her sunken face
A few unstable filaments of hair . . .

As she sprawls on the beach,
Her huge concrete breasts exposed
Above sand, the rest buried underneath,
With siren-nipples wired
To a mesh bikini of transformers.

She will turn and reverse
Nature in her glowing ovum,
The pulse heightened by her sprawled thighs
Whose sinewy voltage cables
Now twine the cities in a leering squat.

O pray that she shall always drown
Her burning in these lead-lined domes
The oceans cool . . . and never birth,
In the savage half-life of the dawn,
That clear worm fathered by equations.

Pray that split neutrons spawned
In her rod-lattice shall hold, hold.
Densities and frictions, shield us!
For Lust, which raised these hardened cones,
Overreached the flesh it faked

In these searing curves, this centrifuge-throat.
O trebly hooped and welded hips of power!
And so our error, which was locked
In shelves of black sea shale,
Unleashed a womb-furnace, a new Moloch.

Night High above the Los Angeles Basin

This coast of yellow streetlamps musters
A grid-like mirror of the star-clusters.

Christmas Shopping at Horton Plaza

novus ordo seclorum

Through teal banners on pink terraces,
Store-fans blow an evergreen perfume
To draw me off the wide outdoor walk
Where built-in speakers maul a Bach fugue . . .

But I prefer to wade through hedges,
Pruned as deer, that haul poinsettia-sleds
Below stucco neo-rotundas
That crown burger and bikini dens.

As a phalanx of Santas throws mints
To hoarse children, who run between floors
Fighting for pieces, while mothers pass
And shop, drifting in and out of stores . . .

An intercom bursts the muzak *Mass
In B Minor* to hail "Sales Events!"
Three seasons pale before the squander
Of these, the final days of purchase.

It is Sabbath. The transactions rise
From high boutique chancel to cart-stall.
The eye of God peers from its dollar,
On each indulgence bought at the mall.

As I stroll and sing an ad-jingle
A plane, towing brand-names, blocks the sun.
One mall-guard, at a gourmet display,
Scares off beggars by tapping his gun.

But why worry? These poor shall settle,
Find jobs, the escalators, good beer,
Having seen the choices, row on row,
Promised. For even they were drawn here.

Someday they too shall browse, and dizzy
With the debts they made in paradise,
Shall know, by name, what these bright columns
Support. Now there is no other life.

They too shall worry, not for clean hearts
But credit ratings, on sleepless nights
And shop all day, helped by thin ladies
Who know its healing, as acolytes.

The sun, stuck at noon, in tanned streaks
Typecasts each palm, each trendy gay,
Among the boulevard boutiques.
Crushed white velvet and *feng shui*.

These perfect girls behind glass counters,
These department store debutantes,
Size me up for sales commission
By the color of my credit cards.

Zone

(after Apollinaire)

At last you are tired of this ancient world.

Eiffel Tower, O shepherd, your flock of bridges
Bleats this morning.

And you are done with living
In this Greek and Roman antiquity.

Here, even the automobiles seem old.
Only religion has remained religion,
Has stayed simple like hangars at the airport.

You are not old: O Christianity!
The Pope is the most modern European
And you, shamefaced beneath the church windows,
Who would not dare to confess this morning.
You read the crying catalogs and posters,
Which are poetry. And for prose, the papers.
For a quarter, you buy detective stories,
Postcards, or a thousand different titles.

This morning, I saw a street for call-girls
Blown clean by the sun. It was a bugle.
Chairmen, office workers, gorgeous stenographers

Passed by Monday through Friday.
Each morning, the factory sirens wailed
And a raging clocktower abolished noon.
The advertising billboards and murals
Screamed, like parrots, their silly commercials.
I love this charming industrial street,
Located on the outskirts of Paris.

In this young street again you are a child.
Mother has dressed you in your Sunday clothes,
Quite small and pious, loving church pomp,
And with your oldest friend, René Dalize.
Later, at night, you escape from the dorms
To pray for hours in the college chapel
While, awesome and ageless like amethyst,
Revolves the flaming glory of the Christ.

This is the gorgeous lily we all touch.
The red-maned torch no wind can extinguish.
The pale-faced son of a grieving mother.
The gallows tree, black with everyone's prayer.
It is the six-pointed star of David.
The god who died and rose three days later.

You walk alone in crowds, now, through Paris
As herds of public buses groan nearby.
And love's miseries grip, like a garrote
Around your throat, and can you love again?

In the old days, you would become a monk;
But here you are ashamed to say a prayer.
You laugh, and your laughter bursts like hellfire;
Its sparks gild your life's abyss.

Today, the women are bloodstained in Paris.

It was (I would rather not remember)
During this slow decline that Our Lady,
Surrounded by her fervent flames, found me
On the hilltop church of Montmartre
And flooded me, so sick of happy words,
With blood from the font of the Sacred Heart.
And that image possesses you, saving
You through insomnias and battlefields.

And now you are near the Riviera
Under lemon trees which always blossom,
Taking boat rides with friends from the country;
Looking down, in fear, at an octopus
Crawling the pearl-gray sea-bottom . . .
As fish symbols swim amid the algae
Bearing the Greek letters of our Savior.

On the edge of Prague, at the inn garden,
A rose on the table, and you are joyous.
You watch, instead of writing in prose,
A rosebug asleep in the heart of the rose.

Outlined in the agates of Saint Vitus,
You almost sobbed to death one day
Like Lazarus, stunned, shaken by the light.
The hands of the ghetto clocks turned backward,
As you turned backward slowly through your life.

Again, you are in Marseilles amid fields
Of watermelons.

Again, at the Hotel of the Giant
In Coblenz.

Again, under the Japanese sour-apple trees
In Rome.

Again, Amsterdam and that hog-faced girl,
And you the only fool to think her pretty.
And that Dutch student that she would marry.
We stayed three days and three more at Gouda.

How many sorrowful, how many happy trips
Before one sees the world grow old!
At twenty and thirty, you fell in love.
Now you don't dare look at your hands,
Since, at any time, you might start sobbing.
Sobbing for whom? For who was it you loved?
And why were you so frightened by nothing?

I lived like a fool and wasted my life.

You stand at the zinc counters of cheap bars
And sip coffee with the other sinners.

You stare at the women in dark restaurants.
The policeman's daughter from Jersey
With the hard and chapped hands, never pretty,
And the abortion scars on her stomach,
Which summon all your pity . . .

You humble your mouth on this bargain whore
With a disfigured laugh.

Alone again, and the dawn is coming
As milkmen rattle their cans in the streets.

Now drink this drink, this burning liqueur—
Like your life, the dregs of the final cup.

You want to walk home, and you begin to.
And there you will find the standard idols,
All those false Christs to muffle the absence.

Good-bye, good-bye.

And then the sun was severed . . .

As Mammon proclaimed a plague
Of lawsuits, the oceans ran red
With tape, while signatures of blood
Appeared on every contract . . .
And then the locusts came
In black columns of print,
In sheet upon sheet of gossip,
Cast down as one consuming tongue
While the prophets, lobotomized,
Swayed, swayed in Bedlam . . .
All stolen from street corners
Where they thumped their Bibles
And were hissed . . . as advertising
Reconciled the people
To Apocalypse . . . the Dragon drew
A third of the stars from heaven,
But spared the satellites
So that men awaited a sign
From TV, entertained to the end.

Near the Suburbs of Alamogordo, New Mexico

On the interstate at noon,
Condominiums flare
From a bleak desert dune.

Nearby, at the heat's crisis,
A dust storm swirls, inflates
Like real estate prices

As the new aqueduct rakes
Mowed lawns from the fused sand
Of the Trinitite lakes.

But these towns remain mirage
And all is desert, filled
By cactus or garage

Since the emptiness endures
In uniformed faces
Behind cash registers

With their mobile homes on blocks,
All seduced to that plain
Where the clock never stops.

As if, colonized, the test-site
Where the fire was unleashed
From the atom's chained flight

Returned, at the end of time,
In one vast sun, which burned
The abyss through every eye.

Deus Ex Machina

As latex gloves install the plastic hearts
That pump gene-spliced plasma to flesh
Fueled by pills to keep psychic parts
From fragmenting in labeled days to death . . .

A hydraulic vice taps and strikes water
From rock, diamond from lumped black coal,
As miracle-tipped pistons stir
To stamp, assembly-line, the sacred mold.

Here, time is kept by the launch code and fuse.
Here, science is a liturgy
And death, a white formula they use.

Was this not the day that was prophesied?
And so a calculating beast
Must come and rule that every future lied.

I wake in a glass-walled ranch house,
And watch golfers concoct half-swings
Then limp across my view, their course
Obscured by sea gray threads of fog,
As trembling deer, through sprinkler rings,
Line the green fairway, chewing sod,
While I stumble from fax to phone:
Committing the small transaction
And endless muddle of the drone.

The screen of my computer clogged
With web-sites and junk mail,
And anything I want to buy:
Swedish cars, Swiss chocolates,
Asian child-brides, British harlots . . .
Each price plus tax. On sale. On sale.

Through the square picture windows, all
Seems at fingertip, clear and free.
The Kingdom of Heaven is near,
Or its facsimile.

I walk outside my fence to find
The blurred shrieking of the blue jays,
The morning newspaper arrived
With its fudged surveys and straw polls,
Its horoscope witches,
Its ad-smudged editorials . . .

Each section spreads its phony gospel.
All stock shares up, and questions cured,
All deaths banished to the back page,
The classifieds and dogmas blurred . . .
Progress in everything.
      I stay inside for days
With three televisions always talking,
Almost the Boy in the Bubble,
Almost sure in such surroundings
That the break must surely come:
The power surge in the machine.
Waiting and, always, awaiting
A glitch in the millennium . . .
      The screen's bleached voice-greeting.
My computer says "hello" and "good-bye."
Through the glass, does something see me?
I'm not sure that it matters why
The lamps turn on and off by touch,
The gadgets freeze into lockstep,
Or how even the blue jays know
That time is short.

While Reading the Revelation of St. John the Divine, I Turn On the Television

How can one name this evil age?

Or say, "Fifty black briefcases
Are missing in Russia. In each,
A small hydrogen bomb . . ."

A brief news-flash, a bulletin.
"A general says that some were sold
To Iraq and to Syria."

Each day, the world holds by a hangnail.

The pasty-faced announcer nods.
"And now, a word from our sponsors . . ."
Will the great and terrible day

Of the Lord hold for commercials?
Heaven's Gate, Waco, Aum Shinrikyo.
And a great star fell from heaven . . .

Which, in Russian, means *Chernobyl.*

I bow and kneel.
How I no longer wish to see
Signs and wonders!

I know better,
But pray that the portents are wrong
And lock the doors . . .

And then the fourth angel sounded.

*Ich habe einmal, und vielleicht mit Recht, gesagt: Aus
der früheren Kultur wird ein Trümmerhaufen und am
Schluß ein Aschenhaufen werden, aber es warden
Geister über der Asche schweben.*

Delayed the airport screens blink.
I sit on this plastic chair, an intruder
To a Jew, no more than fourteen,
Playing *Doom* on his laptop computer.

The rest of this restless crowd rouse
To watch the Lakers trounce the Suns,
While I peruse the essays of Karl Kraus.
Not again, such elegance and diction.

The TV turns and touts the next "great film"
To be a novel, soon, from the screenplay.
I no longer understand this world.
One cannot buy the letters of Gautier.

What became of the past and its riches?
Who built the world that our elders disdained?
"Amidst the crumbling of arts, religions,
Only the stacks of banknotes remain."

A copy of *Time* tops *Reader's Digest*
On a briefcase. Prose for the *littéraire*.

The Dead Sea Scrolls are suppressed.
Vivaldi, synthesized, churns in the air.

That world is passing, or has passed.

No one else is reading but one lady,
Born mocking the machines of Bell and Ford.
Now, as if punished for being early,
A flight attendant shadows her on board.

She leaves, a smiling reproach to the age,
And as ignored as my old professor
Who knew that TV would destroy the page,
As the telephone destroyed the letter.

I have turned twenty-five and obsolete.
The future grinds on, but it is enough
To stand against the age, and such defeat,
With a sneer. A modicum of disgust.

From Homer to Hardy, the pillars stand
Translated, exegesized, and ignored
By mere children who rule here and command
The bread and circus, the barbarous horde.

From my few books, my poor education,
I survey it all from a glacial height

And I, knowing no Greek and less Latin,
But given the robed power to indict . . .

History now belongs to the vanquished.

Once, Lord Swift and Voltaire matched wits.
Once, Auden coined eight hundred words.
Today, the brash are busy writing scripts
For commercials, for advertising blurbs.

Now, box-office receipts form our Bulfinch
As the weekly sitcoms form our fables.
Now, we have old episodes for classics
With glory ranked by the ad-rate tables.

Listen to our shibboleths.
Listen to what our children want to be.
Learn to maximize profits.
Deliver the product effectively.

Gone, the old men with beautiful manners
And all of those in whom tradition lives.
Gone, the last foundations, and the banners,
And with them all the dates, the differences . . .

As darkness chokes the West, and enthrones night
In our scattered schools and shuttered steeples,

Everything de Tocqueville wrote was right:
" . . . on earth, the most prosaic of peoples."

Et aurum est commune sepulchrum.

Shall some Jonah be disgorged from these gates?
Arise from where the businessmen huddle?
Arise from the endless aisles of plane-seats,
Sent by God to warn a stiff-necked people?

No. The crowds are restless but sense no wrong
Inside this terminal, this plush abyss.
The wait is over. Planes roar and throng;
And the day comes, glowing like a furnace.

And I believe that I might understand
Why we shuffle and crowd on board in line;
Why our pilots, steered by machine-command,
Would fly these willing slaves to Babylon.

But nothing shall stand against such progress.
For we are not the men our fathers were,
Who could set back the frontier of darkness.
I shall be the designated mourner.

Out on the tarmac, the ground-crew now pulls
Our plane to leave upon the coming dawn.
I see the end near, the flashing signals,
As that last man, crossing the Rubicon.

Notes

Annexation of Case 40-61

The case number 40-61 refers to Adolph Eichmann's trial in Jerusalem.

The Art of Drifting through Los Angeles

"The Parisian Situationists . . . developed the idea of psycho-geographical derive, a drifting in which the observer hoped to subvert the organization of the capitalist environment by wandering randomly through the urban landscape. By not conforming to the planners' intentions . . . they hoped to free the unconscious within it and to restore vitality and imagination to soulless landscapes."—Elizabeth Young, *Shopping in Space,* 23

Aubade

A lover addresses his inflatable doll.

Deus Ex Machina

deus ex machina [god from the machine] 1. in ancient plays, a deity brought in by stage machinery to intervene in the action . . . hence 2. any character or happening artificially, suddenly, improbably introduced to resolve a situation.

Terminal Diagram

The epigraph is from Ludwig Wittgenstein: "I have said, perhaps rightly: from the earlier culture there is only a heap of rubble and ash, but there are ghosts still hovering over the ashes."

Ultramodern

The epigraph is from Tacitus: "They make a wilderness, and call it peace."

Zone

When I use the word *after* below the title of a poem, what follows is not a translation but an imitation that should be read as though it were an original English poem, to quote Robert Lowell. Approximately a fourth of the original is missing.

Garrick Davis is the founding editor of the *Contemporary Poetry Review*. He has also served as the literature specialist of the National Endowment for the Arts in Washington, DC. His poetry and criticism have appeared in the *New Criterion, Verse*, the *Weekly Standard*, and *McSweeney's*. He is the editor of *Praising It New: The Best of the New Criticism*.